Cheetahs

Victoria Blakemore

For Alison and Clive, with love. It's not quite Norwegian

forest cats, but it's close.. right?

Table of Contents

What Are Cheetahs?

Cheetahs are large mammals. They are members of the cat family. Their name comes from the Hindi word for "spotted one."

Cheetahs are known for being the fastest land mammal on Earth.

They are tan, yellow-orange,

and beige in color. They are

covered in black spots.

Size

Adult cheetahs can be over seven feet long. This includes their tail, which can be up to three feet long.

Cheetahs often weigh between eighty and 150 pounds when they are fully grown.

Male cheetahs are larger and weigh more than female cheetahs.

Physical Characteristics

Cheetahs have claws that help them grip the ground as they run. They have slim bodies with a long tail. These features allow them to run very fast.

Their dark spots work as **camouflage**. They allow cheetahs to sneak up on prey without being seen.

Cheetahs have black stripes that run from their eyes to the end of their jaw. They reduce glare from the sun so they can see better.

Habitat

Cheetahs are usually found in savannas. They prefer areas with long grasses so they can blend in.

They are also sometimes found in the desert. It can make hunting prey harder because they can't blend in.

Range

Most cheetahs are found in the central parts of Africa. They are also found in some parts of Asia

The country of Namibia has the

largest population of wild

cheetahs.

Diet

Cheetahs are **carnivores**. This means that they only eat meat.

Their diet is made up of animals such as antelope, hares, gazelle, and wildebeest.

Cheetahs are very good

hunters because their spots let

them blend into the grasses.

Their fast speed and ability to turn quickly helps cheetahs catch most of the animals that they chase.

Cheetahs usually have to eat their catch quickly. Larger predators like lions have been known to steal their food.

Cheetahs are able to go

several days without drinking

water.

Communication

Cheetahs use sound and scent to communicate with each other. They have a special scent that they use to mark their **territory**. It tells other cheetahs that the area is taken.

They can make sounds like barks, growls, hisses, purrs, and a high-pitched chirping sound.

Cheetahs cannot roar. It does

not have the special bone in its

neck that allows the big cats to

roar.

Movement

Cheetahs are the fastest land mammal. They have been **observed** running at speeds of up to 75 miles per hour.

They have the **ability** to jump and turn in mid-air. They are the only large can that can do this.

The shape and strength of a cheetah's body allow it to run at very fast speeds. This makes them very good hunters.

Solitary Life

Most cheetahs are **solitary** animals. They spend most of their time alone. Sometimes brothers live together, but this does not happen very often.

They are **diurnal**, which means they are most active during the day.

Cheetahs have been known

to rest in trees when it is too

hot.

Cheetah Cubs

Cheetahs have a **litter** of between two and four cubs.

Cubs have a long patch, or mantel, of dark hair down their back. It works as **camouflage**. Their mother also moves them often to keep them safe from predators.

Cheetah cubs spend the first
two years of their lives with their
mothers.

Lifespan

Cheetahs are fully grown by the time they are between two and three years old. They will be able to hunt and take care of themselves by then.

Cheetahs usually live between ten and twelve years in the wild.

Cheetah cubs do not always survive. They are often hunted by larger predators.

Population

In 1900, there were over 100,000 cheetahs in the wild. Now, there are thought to be about 7,000.

About 2,500 of the remaining cheetahs are found in the country of Namibia.

Cheetahs in Danger

Cheetahs are currently **endangered**. There are not many left in the wild.

They have been hunted for sport and for their fur. They are now protected by law, but there are **poachers** who still hunt cheetahs.

Cheetah habitats are being destroyed for buildings and farmland.

Helping Cheetahs

Groups like the Cheetah Conservation Fund are working to help wild cheetahs.

One of the main ways they are helping cheetahs is through habitat **conservation**. They want to make sure cheetahs have a safe place to live.

They also research cheetahs to learn more about them. Learning more about cheetahs can help us to protect them.

Some groups also work with villagers who live near cheetah habitats. They want to help people and cheetahs live peacefully together.

Glossary

Ability: being able to do something

Camouflage: when an animal uses their color to blend in with their surroundings

Carnivore: an animal that eats only meat

Conservation: keeping something from waste or loss

Diurnal: active during the day

Endangered: at risk of becoming extinct

Litter: a group of animals born at the same time

Observed: noticed or seen

Poacher: someone who hunts animals against the law

Solitary: living alone

Territory: an area of land that an animal claims as its own

About the Author

Victoria Blakemore is a first grade

teacher in Southwest Florida with a

passion for reading.

You can visit her at

www.elementaryexplorers.com

Also in This Series

Gray Wolves	Sloths	Flamingos	Camels	Koalas	Honey Bees	Pandas
Pangolins	White-Tailed Deer	Orcas	Giraffes	Corn	Meerkats	Echidnas
Walruses	Raccoons	Bald Eagles	Apples	Arctic Foxes	Red Pandas	Cassowaries
Tigers	Ladybugs	Moose	Beluga Whales	Leopards	Elephants	Jellyfish
Binturongs	Lions	Dolphins	Reindeer	Hammerhead Sharks	Hippos	Pumpkins
Peafowl	Chameleons	Florida Panthers	Aye-Ayes	Black Bears	Cheetahs	Manatees
Gingerbread	Polar Bears	Hot Chocolate	Orangutans	Coyotes	Marshmallows	Strawberries

Elementary Explorers

Victoria Blakemore

Also in This Series

Aardvarks	Mako Sharks	Alligators	Frogs	Hedgehogs	Brown Bears	Bongos
Sea Turtles	Quokkas	Muskrats	Zebras	Red Foxes	Ring-Tailed Lemurs	Platypuses
Anteaters	Kangaroos	Rhinos	Jaguars	Wombats	Capybaras	Gorillas
Cats	Skunks	Butterflies	Dingoes	Snow Leopards	African Wild Dogs	Penguins
Whale Sharks	Wolverines	Warthogs	Caracals	Badgers	Seals	Hummingbirds
Pikas	Humpback Whales	Pumas	Lemonade	Llamas	Tulips	Ostriches
Sunflowers	Fennec Foxes	Sea Lions	Squirrels	Roses	Porcupines	Ice Cream

All titles credited to Victoria Blakemore, Elementary Explorers series.

www.ingramcontent.com/pod-product-compliance
Lightning Source LLC
Chambersburg PA
CBHW051251020426
42333CB00025B/3156